MI'KMAQ

Heather Bruegl

21st Century Junior Library

Indigenous Peoples of North America

Published in the United States of America by:

Cherry Lake Press
2395 South Huron Parkway, Suite 200, Ann Arbor, Michigan 48104
www.cherrylakepress.com

Reading Adviser: Beth Walker Gambro, MS, Ed., Reading Consultant, Yorkville, IL
Content Adviser: Killa Atencio, Mi'gmaq/Quechua

Photo Credits: © Killa Atencio, Photo by Felix Atencio-Gonzales, cover, title page; © Norman Barrett/Alamy, 5; © AP Photo/Robert F. Bukaty, 6; © Tom Ridout/Alamy, 9; © FORGET Patrick/Alamy, 10-11; © meanderingemu/Alamy, 12; © Frank Fichtmueller/Shutterstock, 14; © ZUMA Press, Inc./Alamy, 17; © Irene Abdou/Alamy, 18-19; © Fred J. Field, 21

Cherry Lake Press is an imprint of Cherry Lake Publishing Group.

Library of Congress Cataloging-in-Publication Data has been filed and is available at catalog.loc.gov

Cherry Lake Publishing Group would like to acknowledge the work of the Partnership for 21st Century Learning, a Network of Battelle for Kids. Please visit Battelle for Kids online for more information.

Printed in the United States of America

Note from publisher: Websites change regularly, and their future contents are outside of our control. Supervise children when conducting any recommended online searches for extended learning opportunities.

About the Cover and Content Adviser: Killa Atencio is a poet, artist, and cultural advisor. Originally from Listuguj First Nation in Quebec, she is proud of her Mi'gmaq and Quechua ancestry. Her work includes youth and community development as well as Indigenous relations and education. Her artworks have appeared in exhibitions throughout the Maritimes, including three exhibitions at the Art Gallery of Nova Scotia.

Cherry Lake Press

CONTENTS

WHO WE ARE

The Mi'kmaq and their ancestors have lived on the northeast coasts of North America for more than 13,000 years. They are an Indigenous people with communities in both Canada and the United States. They share culture and language. *Mi'kmaq* comes from the word *nikmaq*, meaning "my kin-friends" in the Mi'kmaw language. The Mi'kmaq call themselves *L'nu*, which means "the people." They call their language *Mi'kmawi'simk* or *Lnuismk*.

EVERY
CHILD
MATTERS

The Mi'kmaq are part of a larger group known as the Wabanaki **Confederacy**, a powerful alliance along the Atlantic coast. Other nations of this confederacy include the Abenaki, the Wolastoqiyik, the Passamaquoddy, and the Penobscot.

Tribal leaders from nations in the Wabanaki Confederacy gather in Augusta, Maine.

Think!

Why would a confederacy be helpful for groups of nations? What do you think they could do together?

The Mi'kmaq honor their connection to the land and sea. They seek to live in harmony with Mother Earth, who gives life and provides food. They believe the Great Spirit, *Kji-Niskam*, is everywhere and in everything. They also believe that all things and all people are connected. Their core values include respect, stewardship, generosity, and honor.

The idea of *Netukulimk* guides Mi'kmaw beliefs and practices. It means understanding and respecting that all things are connected. The message of *Netukulimk* is to take only what you need, leaving a balance for the next **seven generations**.

Make a Guess!

What year will it be seven generations from now? Make a guess! A generation is usually about 25 years long. What might life be like then?

OUR LIVES TODAY

The largest Mi'kmaw population lives in Canada along the Atlantic coast and on the island of Newfoundland. Of the more than 68,000 Mi'kmaq, only about 1,500 live in the United States. Canada has 31 **reserves** where many Mi'kmaq live. In the United States, Mi'kmaq Nation is in northeastern Maine.

Look!

Look at the image. How can you tell that this is a modern-day image? What traditions do you see?

Mi'kmaq may also live anywhere in North America or around the world. Many serve or have served in the Canadian or U.S. militaries. Mi'kmaw men and women are important parts of Canadian and American life. They are teachers, doctors, engineers, scientists, artists, actors, and leaders.

Gordon Sparks is a Mi'kmaw sculptor, shown here working on an ice sculpture in Dartmouth, Nova Scotia, Canada.

Ask Questions!

What questions do you have about how Mi'kmaq are keeping their culture strong? Find a librarian, teacher, or adult to help you find answers to your questions.

Loretta Gould is a Mi'kmaw artist from Cape Breton in Nova Scotia, Canada. She describes her works as spiritual and uses bright colors and bold imagery.

Dr. Albert Marshall is a Mi'kmaw elder, advisor, and teacher. He developed the idea of "Two Eye Seeing," which brings together **aboriginal** knowledge and modern science. It means learning both Indigenous teachings and scientific findings to have a clearer understanding of the world.

Mi'kmaw people everywhere work to keep their culture and people strong.

Newfoundland, Canada, is part of the ancestral lands of the Mi'kmaq.

OUR ANCESTRAL LANDS

The traditional and current lands of the Mi'kmaq are called Mi'kma'ki. They stretch along the Atlantic Ocean in Canada and the United States. Mi'kma'ki includes areas that are now New Brunswick, Nova Scotia, Newfoundland, Prince Edward Island, and Quebec's Gaspe coast in Canada and the state of Maine in the United States.

The traditional **foodways** of the Mi'kmaq included fishing, hunting, and gathering. They hunted large game such as moose and caribou. They harvested food from the sea such as fish and shellfish. They gathered berries and other edible plants when in season. Gathering and hunting food items while they were in season helped protect the land. It allowed the Mi'kmaq to live in balance with nature.

Today, Mi'kmaw **advocates** fight for their rights to the land. Many policies and laws try to stop the Mi'kmaq from hunting or fishing. Mi'kmaw communities in Canada have a **constitutional** right to hunt, fish, and gather. The Mi'kmaq continue to fight for these rights.

Mi'kmaw and other First Nations activists protest abuse of natural resources.

Climate change affects everyone today. Rising sea levels are causing **coastal erosion**. This threatens land, communities, and **sacred** sites. The Mi'kmaq are working to protect the land and keep the environment safe for the next seven generations.

CARRYING TRADITIONS FORWARD

Mi'kmaq have a strong and vibrant culture. Drumming, singing, dancing, and storytelling are important to them. They come together for an annual *Mawiomi*. This means "Gathering" in the Mi'kmaw language. The *Mawiomi* brings Mi'kmaq people together in celebration and joy. They play games, sing, and dance the *Kojua*, a traditional social dance.

In the United States, Mi'kmaq Nation in Presque Isle, Maine, operates a community farm and fish **hatchery**. Fish are an important traditional food, but local waterways were becoming **polluted**. The fish there were not safe to eat. The hatchery provides healthy protein for Mi'kmaw citizens. Each year, it produces 12,000 pounds (5,443 kilograms) of fish.

In Canada, the Mi'kmaw Kina'matnewey **collective** is working to promote Mi'kmaw education and the Mi'kmaw language. Chief Leroy Denny is the chair of Mi'kmaw Kina'matnewey. He says, "Our language is at the heart of who we are as Mi'kmaq."

By working together to solve problems, Mi'kmaq are keeping their traditions alive and strengthening their communities.

Create!

Find out about local community farms or hatcheries in your area. Create an ad promoting one of those places. Include its name and address, what it offers, and how people can support it.

GLOSSARY

aboriginal (a-buh-RIH-juh-nuhl) of or descended from the earliest known inhabitants of a place

advocates (AD-vuh-kuhts) people who speak or act in favor of something

coastal erosion (KOH-stuhl ih-ROH-zhuhn) wearing of Earth's surface by wind or water on a shoreline

collective (kuh-LEK-tiv) a group

confederacy (kuhn-FEH-duh-ruh-see) a group of people or nations joined for a common purpose

constitutional (kahn-stuh-TOO-shuhn-uhl) relating to a nation's organizing laws and principles, usually found in an official written document

foodways (FOOD-wayz) the food practices of a people, region, or historical period

hatchery (HA-chuh-ree) a place for hatching bird or fish eggs

polluted (puh-LOO-ted) made unclean or unhealthy

reserves (rih-ZERVZ) legally designated areas of land for Indigenous peoples in Canada

sacred (SAY-kruhd) holy; important to a system of belief

seven generations (SEH-vuhn jen-er-AY-shuhnz) an Indigenous principle that says all decisions should benefit the next seven generations

FIND OUT MORE

Books

Marshall, Elder Albert D., Louise Zimanyi, and Emily Kewageshig. *Walking Together/Menaqaj Pemwije'tulti'k.* Toronto, Canada: Annick Press, 2025.

Pellissier-Lush, Julie, and Laurie Ann Marie Martin. *Mi'kmaq Campfire Stories of Prince Edward Island.* Charlottetown, Prince Edward Island, Canada: Acorn Press, 2020.

Sorell, Traci. *We Are Still Here! Native American Truths Everyone Should Know.* Watertown, MA: Charlesbridge, 2021.

Online

With an adult, explore more online with these suggested searches.

- "Mi'kmaq Culture," ArcGIS Storymaps
- "Spirituality and Religious Beliefs of the Mi'kmaq," ArcGIS Storymaps

Say Hello!

Kwe' (KWAY) is a way to say "hi" in the Mi'kmaw language.

INDEX

ABOUT THE AUTHOR

Heather Bruegl, a member of the Oneida Nation of Wisconsin/Stockbridge-Munsee, is a Madonna University graduate with a Master of Arts in U.S. History. She is a public historian and decolonial educator, and her Munsee name is Kiishookunkwe, meaning "Sunflower in Full Bloom." Heather frequently travels to present on Indigenous history, policy, and activism, bringing her deep knowledge and personal connection to the subject.